FOUR STEPS
TO BEING A
MORE CREATIVE
YOU

FOUR STEPS
TO BEING A
MORE CREATIVE
YOU

Goose Your Muse Tips for Creatives Series

Y J Kohano

K
E

Nanokas Press

A Division of Kochanowski Enterprises

FOUR STEPS TO BEING A MORE CREATIVE YOU
Goose Your Muse Tips for Creatives Series

Nanokas Press/KE Press books may be ordered through booksellers or by contacting:

Kochanowski Enterprises/Nanokas Press
PO Box 1274
Clackamas, OR 97015-9594
www.yvonnekohano.com
yvonne@yvonnekohano.com

Cover design: John Kochanowski

ISBN:
978-1-940738-10-9 (e)
978-1-940738-11-6 (sc)

Nanokas Press First Edition: 09-06-2016

Contents

FOUR STEPS
TO BEING A
MORE CREATIVE
YOU

WHY YOU NEED THIS BOOK

FOUR STEPS TO BEING A MORE CREATIVE YOU was written with one intention, to inspire you to collaborate with your inner muse and turn out something you've dreamed about, something creative. If you've selected this book, it's because you know you <u>want</u> to be creative. Maybe you already listen to your muse, but you know you can do <u>more</u>. It's the step between knowing and doing where many of us fall off the creativity cliff and struggle to recover.

> *Being creative is hard work, even while it's fun.*

I'll be the first to tell you that being creative over the long term *in any medium* isn't for the faint of heart. I have spurts of writing time when the torrent of ideas flow so quickly, my fingers can't keep up and I swear smoke wafts off the keyboard. On other days, I stare at the blinking cursor because, despite a surplus of directions I <u>could</u> go, nothing seems to fit.

Writers, artists, musicians – we all complain about the same thing. We never have enough time to create, time when the muse is our cheerleader, egging us on to produce something worthy of our best efforts.

But what if you could train yourself to be creative, no matter what the circumstances? What if you could create on cue and make the most of whatever opportunities you have?

Cue the angels singing 'Halleluiah'!

This book traces creative processes I've learned from productive inspirations in various fields, and from my own experience. But this book isn't about me, or even about all of them.

It's about YOU.

Ready to be more creative? Read on!

WHERE DOES CREATIVITY COME FROM?

"Oh, you were born that way."

"To be creative, I have to work one certain way."

"You're just lucky, because you can…"

Reasons – or excuses? I won't judge, since I've heard them all and probably used each of them until I figured myself out. From these examples and many more I'm sure you can add, it's clear we set up our personal roadblocks to success without even realizing we're doing so. Here are some examples.

A writer friend says that the only way she can work is in total silence. I mean, complete and total, absolute silence. She has a set of what I can only call earmuffs strictly for this purpose. (She calls them noise-cancelling coverage, but they *are* fuzzy on the outside.) They look a little strange in the middle of a hot summer day, but they work for her. While she wears them, she can be productive. Take them away, and she is unable to conjure a single word, distracted by any bright shiny things around her.

Another writer must have his playlist. He spends countless hours crafting THE PERFECT selection of songs he believes most accurately reflect the mood he wants to achieve in his story. He then plays it in a continuous loop, day in and day out, as he writes. If for some reason he has no way to play the music, his pen shakes over the page as he writes nothing.

The sequence of notes needs to be superb, without a single beat out of tune, according to one musician. His work must be flawless from the first note he creates, or his effort is worthless. His anxiety to create performance-ready songs without need for revision means he produces very slowly and very little. What he does write he often throws aside, frustrated when it requires more work. He calls his muse a fickle friend, appearing only rarely and then at inconvenient times.

An artist carries his paints with him everywhere. They have long since left permanent stains on his car's back seat upholstery. People never sit there anyway, crowded by easels and canvases with no room for humans. He never wants to be far away from his creative medium, just in case lightning strikes. Of course, he also says he can only work on a sunny day. Never cloudy, only sunny.

> *We all have ideas, things we want to create.*
> *The difference between creatives and the rest*
> *of the population is that creatives do something*
> *about it.*

The gap between thinking about being creative and doing something about it is can be a deep chasm or a narrow crack – it's our choice. We recite a litany of reasons to ourselves about why our creativity happens within boundaries, but those boundaries are of our own making. We can ALWAYS do something about blowing up those barriers.

I recently met a young woman, age thirteen going on forty, who is a writer. Asked what genres she writes in, she happily replies "Everything". And it's true! Sci-fi, steam punk, suspense, romance – and memoires thrown in for fun. Her journaling produces stacks of notebooks each year. She's worn out the keyboard on the laptop her mother bought her two years ago. She is prolific.

And her secret? She knows no creative boundaries, perhaps because the world hasn't rubbed off on her yet. More importantly, she has not created any barriers in her mind. She can scribble anywhere, and as her parents attest, under any conditions. (Actually, they say when she's writing, an earthquake could tumble the building down and she probably wouldn't notice.)

Wouldn't you LOVE to have that kind of focus for your craft? To my young friend, it's all FUN. Getting to know her made me examine my own inspiration, drive and stamina. I dug deeper into this boundary setting thing, and here's what I learned.

> Our creative flow is more flexible and supple than
> we allow it to be.

CREATIVE RHYTHM

Also known as "being in the zone", creative flow is a psychological concept that emphasizes our hyperfocus on the work in front of us. Being wrapped up in our project to the exclusion of almost anything else (including earthquakes) means our involvement is complete. We find joy and energy in the _doing_, rather than only the end result, and that means we enjoy the creative _process_, the journey from idea to finished work. Imagine this.

> You immerse in your creative mode. Second-
> guessing the value or quality of what you create
> never crosses your mind. Your movements are
> hurried, as fast as you can function. The
> process takes you over, and yet at the same
> time, you control the process. Time loses all
> meaning until you glance up and find day has
> turned into night as your stomach growls, long
> overdue for a meal. Your euphoria as you
> glance back to your work knows no bounds, and
> a smile of intense satisfaction lights your face.

What an awesome creative process! Likened to a religious experience for obvious reasons, the possibility to enjoy this creative flow is in all of us.

There's a catch, though. To be in the flow, other things need to be set aside. According to Mihaly Csikszentmihályi, the researcher credited with identifying the concept of flow in the mid-1970's, our minds process a finite amount of data per second. He states that decoding speech by itself eats up more than half of our finite processing capacity.

That would mean even listening to a television show while working means we cannot create at our full potential capacity. While we may not consciously intend to be hearing the words, our subconscious registers the conversation. We are not thinking about it, but decoding still happens.

On the flip side, though, if we are effective at blocking out the static, even noise filled with words our brains might otherwise <u>want</u> to decode, we can immerse in the flow of our creative process. This doesn't require headphones or blaring music. <u>The focus comes from *inside us.*</u> We target our energy on our task to the exclusion of all else. We are not bored with our work. No fear about lack of skills to complete what is in front of us dissuades us. An end result is our goal, a result we can measure in some way, and we can adjust our progress based on how well we're meeting our goal.

How can you get into your state of creative rhythm? Concentration. The right task. Cultivating your environment. Visualization. In other words, propagate creative energy in your work by not distracting it with anything else to process. More on how to do this in our upcoming four steps.

> *Being creative uses our conscious and subconscious in ways we are not aware of, ways we may not even control.*

SUBCONSCIOUS MIND

We like to think our creative process is a conscious thing, something we can direct and harness at the flicker of synapses. <<SWITCH>>. Ready, set, go.

But we never get off the starting blocks if the message we're REALLY telling ourselves in our subconscious mind is negative. You see, our subconscious doesn't know real from make-believe. Have you heard the phrase, 'Fake it 'til you make it'? Through this make-believe, we train our minds, and most importantly, our subconscious, with the message we will turn into action. **And *our subconscious* is where *our creativity* comes from.**

Countless books have been written about this. They are not only from the artistic world but from sales and marketing, athletic professionals, and entertainment gurus.

What are they doing? Harnessing the subconscious to make their work easier.

For example, one sales expert who has convinced people to buy millions of dollars of items recommends saying, "I like myself," at least thirty times a day. That is 3-0 times. Why? Because if you like yourself, you will come across as more positive, upbeat and convinced of the worth of whatever you sell.

You might think this is crazy, but the people he trains – and there have been thousands of them – have realized proven success through this method. Confidence in yourself communicates to those around you as confidence in your message. And after repeating that phrase over two hundred times a week for a while, your subconscious buys it too!

Professional athletes do this as well, but in another form. They learn to visualize what that next play, competitive course, or physical move looks like. They imagine how they will feel as they take each step to their successful conclusion. This type of role playing happens not just once, but over and over in a variety of combinations.

Have you ever watched a great soccer team on the pitch? Their players don't need to look at each other to pass the ball with accuracy, because not only have they rehearsed the move countless times as a group, they also play it in their minds until it's something they don't need to think about. Subconscious takes over and makes the play for them.

What makes an actor great in a role? He or she convinces us, the audience, that they are the character they portray. We no longer see the big name or new upstart. The character rules. How do they do that? They practice, rehearse, train themselves to think, act and BE that person. When an expression crosses their face, it's believable because their subconscious has been trained to be someone else. No wonder it takes them so long to recover from a performance!

> *Being creative is a journey, not a destination.*

JOURNEYING

Education, experience and existence have trained us to focus on results. Get good grades. Complete those reports. Clean the house, do the laundry, finish the shopping. These are all destinations, but they are not the reason we exist. In a fulfilled and fulfilling creative life, we exist for the 'being', not the 'done'.

Journeys are by definition the act of getting from point A to point B. They measure distances covered, and they are the passage, as in 'journeying'. The status or placement of the beginnings and ends are not important. We take many different kinds – safe journeys, sentimental ones, long ones, last ones. Commonly we also phrase life, love, and success as journeys by themselves.

Creativity is a journey too. We begin with an idea, a concept, a theme. Teasing that out into the final whatever may take hours or years. We might feel like we never reach the destination, or we may still be unsure about reaching it when we do. What we should <u>not</u> do, though, is make the creative journey all about arriving at the end. *Where's the fun in that???*

What you *don't* want is to create for the sake of churning things out. Imagine slopping paint on a canvas because you have a show coming up. You need XX number of pieces to hang at the show. You have XX minus-minus, the show (journey's end) is approaching, and you need lots more to cover those bare walls. Your destination, a 'finished' piece, is what you want. How does it look? Is it the best you are capable of or just okay for right now? Who cares?

I *know* that's not you. (It isn't, right???) You CARE about the work bearing your name. You would no more display a substandard piece than you would parade down Main Street at high noon in nothing but your undies. (Wait, that *wasn't* you, was it???) But when it comes to deadlines and panic, we creatives are creatures of habit. Destination is where we focus, not the journey.

But what if…

What if you focused on the journey, the fun in creating the work, the joy that comes with it? What are the chances that this kind of product will be special, unique, and reflective of your true talent?

AND – don't you think your audience will be able to tell?

SO – phone it in and rush to your destination, producing something (many more somethings) you are not proud of.

OR – *dial it in and focus on the creative process.*
That journey may take us longer on a piece-by-piece basis, but what we then offer our public is so much stronger for the effort.

BEGINNING OUR JOURNEY

In this little chapter, you've thought about harnessing your creative flow, training your subconscious to do what it does best in guiding you, and embracing the importance of the journey that is uplifting creativity. By now, I bet you're itching to try things for yourself, so without further delay, let's get to the steps.

Step 1 – Visualize your best creative life

Step 2 – Ask yourself "Why not?"

Step 3 – Fill your creative well

Step 4 – Employ productive strategies

Gather some big pieces of paper and colored pens or crayons – we're going to get creative right now!

STEP 1 – VISUALIZE YOUR BEST CREATIVE LIFE

It doesn't matter if you cannot *fully* implement your best creative life – yet. For most of us, obligations keep us distracted with other things. Some of those things are pleasant, like the people we love, or contribute to our overall well-being, like earning our lifestyle. That doesn't mean we can't also be creative. The key is finding the life that works *for you*.

Designing your best creative life does not mean you will be able to implement all aspects of it right off the bat. BUT – you have to start somewhere, and that beginning is knowing what you want it to look like. Then, as time and circumstances allow, incorporate little bites of it into your daily routine.

BUT – what if the things we must do to survive appear too insurmountable? A short aside about barriers, the first being day jobs. We generally intend that term to mean the jobs we have to do to earn money to enjoy what we *want* to do. The implication is what we do to earn the bucks gets in the way of our creative life.

This may be true, but only up to a point. We are creatives. The angst of doing whatever we must can be used to fuel our creative fire. As you work on the following exercises, please remember that jettisoning the day job is an unreal expectation for most of us as we start out. Flow with it and make it work for your creative life, not against it.

> *Creativity is part evolution, part devolution, and part revolution.*

The big barrier I hear people mention is family responsibilities. Children, parents, significant others, close friends – they all have a piece of our time. What kind of person would you be, though, if you never felt deep emotions for and with others? Would you be good at the love-and-commitment side of life? Could you be as creative without feelings? Most people I talk to find they would not.

Another barrier is time we set aside for ourselves. When you are creative, you need to stoke the fires that bring you passion, and that is found in more than other people. It's found inside of us, something to be nurtured and treasured. (If I don't write on a regular basis, I get downright crabby!) It's a vital part of us, and probably a major part of why others love us. Feed your creative fire with meaningful, meditative time on a regular basis, and your creative processes will respond positively as an outcome.

Now, back to our fun stuff…

DRAW THE PICTURE

We'll begin our first step by drawing a picture about what we want our creative life to look like. It's not just any ol' picture, either, but THE picture. The dream. This is the first step to making "someday" a reality. Don't get stuck in trying to figure out the how's and what's. Emotions and feelings reign supreme in this stage.

This isn't something you can do on the fly and be done with it, either. No, this takes a few visits to your hidden corners, secret desires and brassy outright WANTS. You'll think about it, add to it, maybe delete something, and finally, finally, you'll think you've got it all down. You won't, but that's part of the creative journey. Revisit it on a regular basis to nurture its growth with new ideas as they occur to you. Be willing to update it when necessary. It is words on a piece of paper, not cast in stone. And even stone can be chiseled into something new!

Subconscious is where our creative lives.

Do you have a hard time thinking about your best creative life? Feel like "real life" weighs so heavily that imagination is scarce? Try thinking about what you'd do if you won the lottery! You know, the big prize with lots of zeros on it. More on my take on this when I tell you the llama story later on...

I like mind-mapping for this exercise, but if you're a list maker, by all means, make lists. Outline if you need to plot things. Collage crazy? Find pictures and phrases. I've taught many people to mind-map over the years, and they all find something positive from the activity. So try it once – for me!

> Creativity is like a muscle – the more you use it, the stronger it can become.

Map Your Dream

The process of mind-mapping is simple. Take any central word or concept. Around it, place as many main ideas or topics that relate to the concept as you need. These are called "child" words. Take each "child" and repeat with subtopics. You can go as far as it makes sense for what you're working on. What you end up with looks like the actual structure of neurons in your brain.

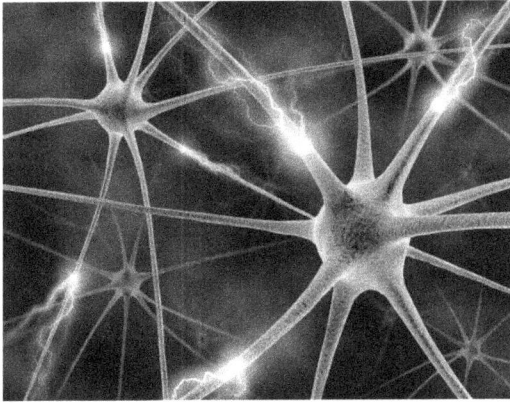

Sidebar time again. Mind-mapping is a great tool to use to brainstorm, take notes, outline, build a research database, organize thoughts for a talk – the ways to use it are only limited by your whims and fantasies. Tony Buzan popularized the radiant thinking and mind-mapping approach around 1990, and it has since been used from universities to corporations to nonprofit systems. Have a complex idea to present and don't know where to start on it? Try a mind-map!

Your Map of Creative Life

Here is where we begin to practice what we're learning. Take out a big piece of paper – or lots of printer paper. The central topic is the main idea you want to tease out. Radiating from that, topics that pertain to the idea are noted.

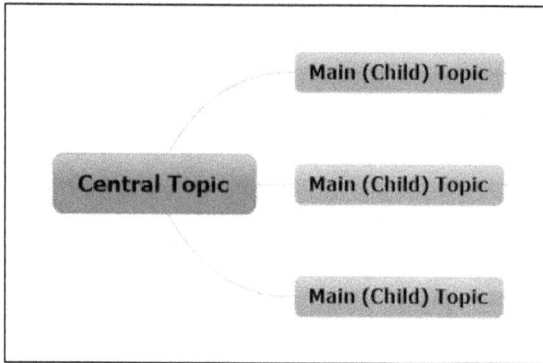

For this exercise, the central topic is "More Creative Me". (If you're using printer paper, either write very small, or put the phrase in a corner and use multiple sheets for each 'child'.)

Next, visualize what your best creative life will look like. (Notice I said 'will', not it's less enthusiastic cousin 'could'. Already, we're training your subconscious to get you to where you want to go.) "What This Looks Like" is a main topic off "More Creative You".

Every person is unique, so your next set of branches/children will be unique to you as well. What components of that creative life do you want to think about? Mine read:

- I am...

- My world is...

- My day holds...

- I do…

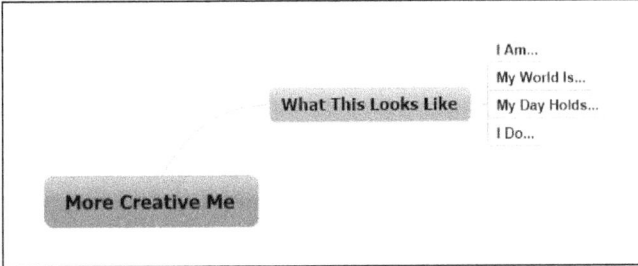

But you could just as easily say lifestyle for things "I do", or health and happiness for "I am". Make it meaningful for you. There is no right or wrong. You are simply visualizing what your best creative life will be like.

Goose Your Thinking

Creativity unleashed is a powerful emotive thing, and we don't always want to explore it. Don't have any ideas about what to include? Ask yourself these questions:

- What do I yearn for?

- If money wasn't an issue (or time or other commitments), what would I do with myself?

- What passion have I never taken the time to realize?

- What activities bring me the most joy?

How many levels or layers can you add to your map of 'what if'? If you want to be your best creative self, you have to allow yourself to DREAM BIG. Go on – who will know? This is FOR YOU!

Here's how you can continue growing this:

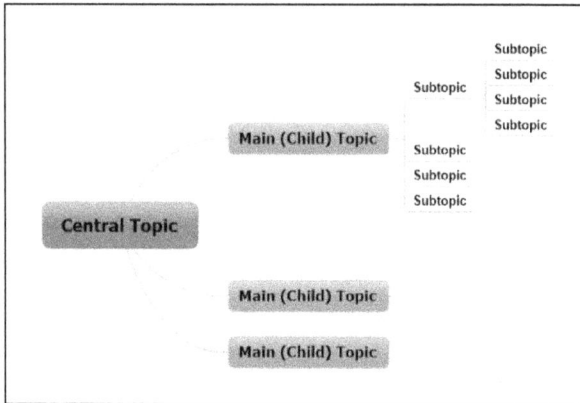

When you've added that first set of branches, keep going. For example, if lifestyle is one of yours, what does that mean? Keep adding further branches until you've gone as far as you want on a topic. I recommend at least two to three levels deep.

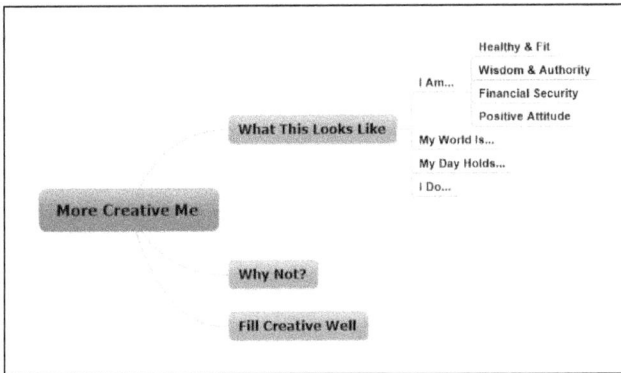

Want a giggle over my scribbles on this first main topic? Promise me you won't laugh, because I am no artist and my handwriting made the nuns at my grammar school cry. But I like colors, so I pulled out an old set of pencils and got to work. Crayons work well too. (I've given boxes of them to rooms full of engineers, doctors and other professionals and you'd be amazed how that childhood trigger opens up doors to our souls!)

Exercise 1: Your Mind-map

Spend time on your mind-map now. Come back here when you have taken at least two branches as far as you can and have run out of ideas. Don't worry, I'll wait!

> *My map means something to me;*
>
> *Yours is for YOU.*

MAPPING AH-HAS

What do you notice about mapping? Did any major realizations jump out at you? I know that when I do this, I find myself second-guessing what I write, and thinking maybe I should be more existential, or maybe more profound. But no, that's not necessary. Someone else's "should" does not matter. The meaning is for me, and as long as it means something in my creative life, that's what matters.

Interpreting a Map

Let's explore what documenting this means. It provides us with a method of gathering and interpreting our thoughts about our creative life. Understanding what motivates us is the first step to *being* motivated. Here are some insights from my map by way of example.

Some of my creative attributes show up at the first level of my map, under "I am". I want to be a good role model, so I want people to practice what I preach (along with me). People tell me I have wisdom about a subject, and they'd like to share it. Part of my creative self is therefore part and parcel of who I am – a storycatcher, teacher and consultant. I came out of the womb that way, and when I die, I'll be trying to fix things on the other side too!

Another important creative part of me is my attitude. I intend to be positive and active in my chosen field. Like most writers, it's my nature to be introverted, to get my creative energy from time by myself. I recognize the importance in filling my creative well from outside sources too, and keeping my well at a healthy level. More later on how I do that. Balancing (*not necessarily staying in balance*) the internal and external facets feed my creative energy in different ways.

What would I like my day as a creative person to look like? More importantly, what are 'real' priorities, and what are distractions? Distractions are defined as things we do because *we think we should*, even if we could really avoid them. Telling ourselves we're <u>too busy</u> is a distraction by itself, a way of hiding behind a to-do list to avoid doing what we really want but are too afraid to try.

Priorities, on the other hand, are what we assign value to. Time with my husband – and by this I mean quality time when we talk without distractions – is of critical importance to me, so I make time for it. You might do the same with your children or friends. (Or pets – I have to be careful, my dogs are reading over my shoulder!)

Ask the Lottery Question

What items listed are possible boundaries or barriers? I'm betting some of your first and second level branches off visualizing your creative life have aspects of both to them. That's normal. We think about what makes us avoid risks rather than what encourages us to take them. Human beings, once more! But recognizing them allows us the understanding to make changes to achieve our creative life.

Let's take another example from my map, "I Do", which to me is lifestyle. What is important to me in my creative lifestyle? This one has continued to be an eye-opener for me over the years. It's the **llama story**.

Years ago, we raised llamas on a ranch in Northern California. We got into it because my husband and I enjoyed backpacking in the wilderness when we were younger, but we no longer wanted to carry big loads for long distances. Llamas make great pack animals and are easy to raise (and love). Believing we could blend business and pleasure, we thought we'd lead backpacking trips into the Sierras, with the critters doing the part our backs no longer liked to do.

It was fun, even as a side business. We both had demanding day jobs, my husband with a long commute each way and me on the road consulting and teaching. Over time, we realized we were doing more _for_ the llamas than _with_ the llamas. That was not the point of this endeavor. (You can see from the picture below, their 'cute' factor was never a question! Mamas and babies...)

Then we asked ourselves an important question. "What if we win the lottery?" (Don't we all dream about that?) Answering honestly, we realized the llamas, while wonderful fuzzy friends and a great distraction, did not play a role in that visualized future. In fact, in some ways, they detracted from it, since travel and lots of it was high on our list of adventures.

The llamas all went to terrific homes, and we enjoyed seeing their progeny at county fairs and local parades. (Sniff!) What's the lesson in this long-winded story? If we hadn't examined our desires for the future, we would not have recognized we were no longer llama ranchers in our hearts. They were no longer part of what we visualized for our future.

Still Struggling?

I understand that it is difficult to figure out what our creatives lives would look like, if we eliminated the barriers and lived with no boundaries. This is both an exciting and scary concept! If you are still struggling to figure out what's important to you, ask yourself:

- If I won the lottery (the big prize), what would my life look like?

- If time was never an issue, how would I spend my creative energy?

- What can I do TODAY to make my life look more like that dream?

This tells you what you would change, given the ultimate opportunity. Recognizing it is the first step to making it happen in real life.

> *Your 'creative' is a place no one else can go –*
> *only you have been there, and only you will*
> *ever bask in its glory.*

If you're *still* having a hard time with this exercise, take a deep breath and a step back. Go to your favorite place to create, and use the tools you use best. Pick up that paintbrush, type an outline, play notes or take a few photos. What does your creative future feel like in your hand? Create the visualization, the stimulus, so you can return to it and embed it in that stubborn subconscious.

STEP 1 ON YOUR JOURNEY

In this chapter, you learned about mind-mapping and why it is useful to capture your vision for your best creative life. I showed you some examples to get you started, and the next steps were up to you.

How do you like the map you've begun? Are you getting excited about implementing your creative life, but are afraid the walls in front of you are too high to climb? No worries! In our next step, we learn how to tear down those barriers.

STEP 2 – ASK YOURSELF 'WHY NOT?'

Why NOT live your best creative life? Okay, come on, give them to me – all of the reasons why you can't embrace it. I'm going to tell you each and every one is an excuse, and you'll hate me for it – before you realize I'm right and love me. This is the time for honesty and lots of it. We're going to knock down walls preventing you from being your best creative self.

To destroy those boundaries and barriers, it first helps to define them. Boundaries are limits we set so that we can only go so far before whatever it is stops us. We walk the path for a while, only to run into a locked gate. Barriers, on the other hand, bring us to a full stop before we even begin. I liken this to a journey we never begin because we can't leave our own front door.

My challenge to you is -

BLOW UP THE BARRIERS!

TEAR DOWN THE BOUNDARIES!

But first, you need to recognize them. Mind-mapping time once again. Here's mine!

What This Looks Like

More Creative Me

Why Not?

TIME	Uncontrollables	Work arounds	
	Work/Life Balance		
	Make vs. Buy		
	Too Many Projects		
	It Takes Too Long to be Discovered		
EDUCATION	Tools		
	Technology		
	$ cost		
	Classes		
	Lifelong learning		
SKILL	Put in the time		
	Practice		
	Maybe not good enough - yet		
	Work habits		
DOUBT	Internal	Not good enough	
		Don't want it badly enough	
		Not practicing daily/regularly	
	External	Lack family/friends support	
		Critics and reviewers	
INFLEXIBILITY	Organized to work		
	Only one way to create		
	Only one way to distribute		
INSPIRATION	Fill the creative well	Subconscious	
		Experiences	
		Quiet time	
	Examine the world		
	Seek ideas	Cutting files	
		Organization	
	What if?		

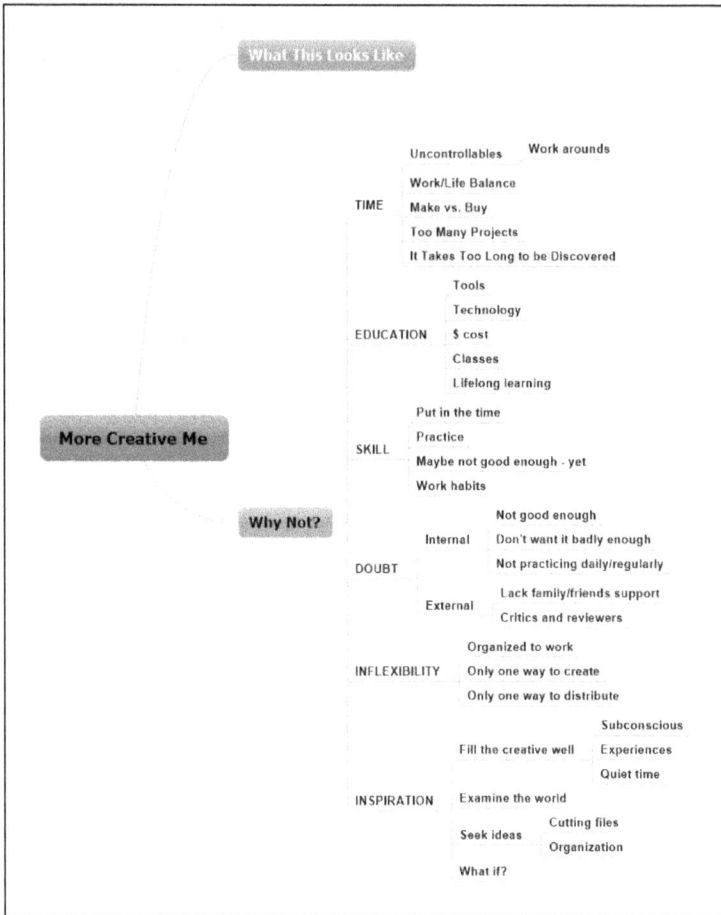

On this branch off your creative center, you capture all of the reasons "Why Not?" Why are you living something other than your creative life? Your reasons will be personal to you. I hear common themes from creatives, and each one fits me. Bet they do for you too!

THE TIME DEMON

Number one bugaboo on my list is TIME. I never feel like I have enough of it, no matter how hard I try to guard it carefully and nurture it as closely as I do tomato seedlings in the spring. When I'm honest with myself, I realize I have more control over this than I think. My subconscious thinks I don't have enough, so I somehow – don't. Self-fulfilling prophesy and all that.

Some of the issues coming up for me are setting legitimate boundaries on my time. For example, I belong to a number of volunteer groups, and you know how that goes. Can you say 'no' when they ask you for help? I have great difficulty doing that. Clearly, I know how to change this – now, for that messy implementation part!

Another is work-life balance. To me, this means having time for the things that are critical and urgent. But first, I need to take a step back to determine if those activities really are important – or is my subconscious fooling me into thinking they are? I can always find a hundred things that 'need' doing. Does anyone (other than me) care if there's a little dust on the furniture?

Let's take a few minutes for a sidebar discussion about balance. I recently heard a great phrase – "Balance is bullshit". The speaker's intention was to point out that balance might occur for a second in time, is difficult to achieve, and was impossible to hold on to for longer than scant seconds. Need proof? Stand up. Get up on your toes, and see how long you can stay there. Unless you're a prima ballerina, I'm guessing you can't do it for long.

And why is that? Skill and training. Doubt. Interest or desire.

We are not super-human, much as we'd like to be. We cannot balance everything. But unless we recognize what we want and why it is important to us, we won't find ways to compensate and make an effort towards a more balanced existence. Like a teeter-totter in motion, we swing from the jarring thump on the ground to flying high, but rarely do we hover in the middle for an indefinite period of time.

> *If you want something badly enough, nothing will hold you back – not a brick wall or a flooded river or rabid self-doubt.*

Back to mind-mapping. I classify time in two broad categories. One is within my control; the other is not. I have to accept the uncontrollable (like the internet repair man arriving a day early when I was on my way out to yoga class) and work around its impact on my life.

The controllable, though, are the things I can truly manage. That's what belongs on my map, so I can develop strategies to manage them.

Controllable items in my world include too many projects. I am blessed with many writing ideas that exceed my bandwidth to produce in the hours in the day. (I have not yet figured a way to make more than twenty-four hours in a day happen. If you do, get on the speaking circuit. *You'll be a gazillionaire.*) You probably have a long list of your own ideas, but never feel like you can implement them all.

I have to prioritize writing projects so that the ones most important to one of my goals – happiness, success, money – are the ones I concentrate on. Some are urgent, like the book I'm writing here. Others, like a story I may or may not ever publish because it wanders and I like it that way, don't even move the critical meter.

How can I manage these competing priorities? After all, I am one person. I can't partition my brain and creative energy in the same way someone can partition a hard drive in a computer to function like two different operating systems. Multitasking means I'm probably doing a less than effective job on everything I'm juggling. Concentrating on one thing at a time is the best way for most of us to get things done.

How can you set aside time for the controllable things? Set priorities – as long as one of them is time for you to be creative! I put that time in my calendar as an appointment with myself. I select the most important writing task of the day – new words or editing – and do that first in my creative time. I repeat this for the second priority item, and so on. Time is no longer a boundary or a barrier, but my friend.

EDUCATION AND SKILL

We have to pay our dues. For ninety-nine-point-nine percent of writers, we don't get discovered with our first book, even if it's a great read. People need to get to know you before you move up the list. The same happens for artists, musicians, entertainers, athletes. That's why education may be a barrier for some of us if we are not willing to practice, practice, practice. For this reason, "Education" (the learning how to do) and "Skill" (the practice to make it my own) are major branches on my map.

If this concept doesn't resonate with you, think about earning a promotion. You may believe you can be great at what you could be doing in that next rung up the ladder, but until you learn the skills in your present position, your chances are weak of being allowed to climb it – yet. You are not ready – and probably rightfully so – and that feels like it is out of our control.

> *You never know what will spark your next creative idea. Be open to learning and be open to trying new things.*

Within our influence, though, is preparation. Being our best creative self doesn't exist in a vacuum. We need to develop our abilities, no matter what medium we're working in. Remember my thirteen-year-old friend and her exuberance about her writing? It shows promise. It's good, and with additional training and practice, she'll be great. A quarterback doesn't throw the perfect spiral without practice. Neither does the stock market analyst recognize the next overachieving winner.

Practice. Study. Rehearsal. Doing it right, over and over, tells our subconscious what needs to be done so we can do it without thinking about it. And once we achieve that, it leaves our conscious mind available to take the next steps. The boundaries are the skills we have developed, while the barrier is not continuing to learn, grow, practice and develop in your creative field.

Another aside from my preachy inner self. I firmly believe in lifelong learning. No matter who you are or what you do in your life, there is always something new to learn. If you deny yourself the pleasure of learning, you have one foot in the grave. Never stop, because when you stop learning, you stop living. Now, back to our book...

BAN SELF-DOUBT

Right now, before you take your next breath, do this. There is NOTHING to keep you from your dreams except inertia. I don't care who you are or how off-course your creative life seems to be, YOU CAN DO IT. It takes time, effort, and commitment. (It may take me the rest of my decades on this planet to become any kind of drawing artist. That doesn't mean I won't try. Maybe I'll start a new art era...)

> *Reasons are just excuses dressed in party clothes.*

Doubt is a CREATIVITY KILLER. Internal doubt sends immediate warnings to our subconscious to step away from whatever it is we consciously want to try. We tell ourselves we're not GOOD enough, but in reality, we don't want it BADLY enough! We can learn to get better. Convincing ourselves we cannot learn anything more will hold us back from everything. Remember, reasons are just excuses dressed in party clothes.

Or, repeat after me – *"I like myself!"* Fake it 'til you make it.

The other brand of doubt is external. Your family-slash-friends dismiss the importance of what you're doing, and you lack formal support. They knock you down. *Get back up.* If they knock you down again, consider finding a new set of friends and jettisoning your relatives! For every time they tell you 'can't', say "YES I CAN" and prove them wrong!

In all seriousness, though, remember that they have doubts too. They might belittle what you do because then they have to face the fact that they aren't living their creative lives either. If you get yours, what will they do? Maybe this is a journey you can achieve side by side, even if you need to walk different types of creative paths.

Doubt from the inside – a barrier that holds you back if you let it. Doubt from those around you – a boundary that might contain you for a while, but only for as long as you allow it. You decide.

INFLEXIBILITIES

The final boundary is inflexibility in work habits, and boy, is this a doozy! Remember my previous stories about 'only one way'? There is no such thing as only one way. We may *prefer* to do things a certain way, but that doesn't mean it's the *only* way. Sometimes, pushing this boundary out of the way – but no, blow this one up completely – lets us emerge with even more creative energy.

I can give you an example from my creative life. I am lucky in that I don't have many things I absolutely can only do one way when it comes to writing. I can write in silence, noise, whatever. I can write in my office, my chair, a ubiquitous coffee shop with a green lady on the cup, an airport, plane, train or automobile (but not while driving). I can use a pen and paper, though I'm much better off with a computer or tablet of some sort. (There is a good reason for this – the aforementioned atrocious handwriting, plus my brain works much faster than my hand can capture, but I type darned fast.)

The one boundary *I thought I had* was my ability to be creative at a set time of the day. For some years, I told myself I did my best work if I wrote first thing in the morning. I decided to push my boundary and try writing at different times of the day. It took some getting used to, like trying to use my left hand for a task when I favor my right, but with practice (gee, that word again), I overcame that message in my subconscious. Now, my subconscious has heard I can write whenever I make the time, including the middle of the night if need be.

And guess what? I can! What stories are you telling yourself about only being able to create "one way"? Tear down that wall! Try something different, and you will probably surprise yourself in wonderful ways.

```
                    What This Looks Like


    More Creative Me                    TIME
                                              +
                                        EDUCATION
                                                +
                                        SKILL
                                             +
                       Why Not?       — DOUBT
                                            +
                                        INFLEXIBILITY
                                                   +
                                        INSPIRATION
                                                 +
```

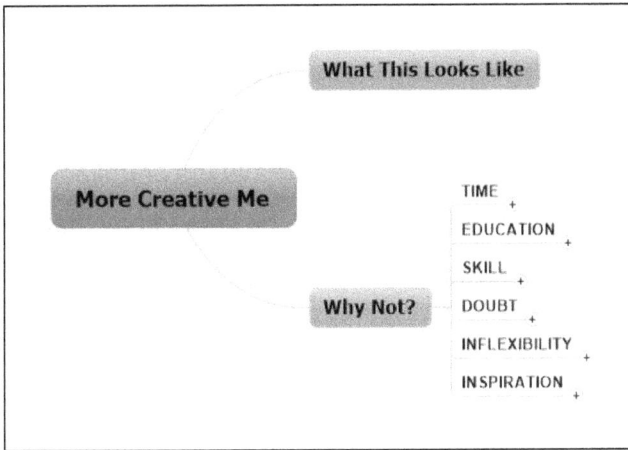

Exercise 2: Your Honest Self-Assessment
Add the things you consider boundaries and
barriers to your mind-map.

Self-assessment is hard, because we (humans again) tend to believe we're either much better or much worse than we really are. In my experience, thinking we're much worse is a plea for recognition from others – or self-doubt. Thinking we're much better masks a poor self-image – or self-doubt. In either case, we act the way we do because we don't want to be found out. Once we're exposed, we'll have to change to either improve or stop denying we're good. Heady stuff, this.

If you feel you can't take an honest look at yourself, ask a handful of trusted friends to help you. I emphasize 'trusted'. Someone who wants to change you into what they want you to be won't be anywhere nearly as helpful!

Next, take a look around your field. Analyze the work of people you admire, your competitors, and those hotshots on the way up. What do they have or do that you don't? You might find some of those things are the uncontrollable, like being discovered or having put in the time to pay their dues. Then again, they must have been prepared when their time came, or they would not be standing in that position today.

Chances are, you'll find gaps between what you have and what you need to have in terms of skills and capabilities. We all do, and since almost every creative field – no, scratch that, I can't think of a single darned creative endeavor that is static. Every artistic field changes on a regular basis, and we need to continue to update our skills. Furthermore, things go in and out of style. Remember cubism? Today, we hate cubes and all they signify, like putting people in boxes!

Once you recognize what you need to update, you can develop a plan. Go ahead, put that on your map. Don't forget the word "practice", or if you prefer, "rehearse". Your subconscious will thank you for it!

What inflexibilities have you convinced yourself of in your creative life? How will you overcome them? And those other boundaries and barriers, what about them? That's what we'll tackle in our next step.

STEP 2 ON YOUR JOURNEY

Self-talk can hurt us by blocking our progress. It can also help us by encouraging our inner language to change. We might freeze into our tracks if someone tells us *we can't* for no good reason, unless we have a dialogue with ourselves that says *we can*. In this chapter, we covered the need to recognize our boundaries and barriers in order to dismantle them. Next, we'll come up with methods to conquer any of these stumbling points so we can continue on a successful best creative life journey.

STEP 3 – FILL
YOUR CREATIVE WELL

Our creativity is endless. The well is bottomless – even when it feels like we've sucked it dry. You see, we can refill it, and much more easily than a physical well of water in a drought. We don't need an atmospheric river we cannot control to flow over us, either. In most cases, we simply need to find things to inspire us in a way that we will not be distracted.

What do I mean by this? We live in age where multitasking is the norm. We drive and listen to audiobooks, or podcasts, or music. We exercise with the same. We walk or run outside with a conversation or headsets. We are rarely alone with our thoughts, and what's more, we rarely empty our minds to allow new things to filter in.

I know, I know. You're a busy person. What you do is IMPORTANT. YOU are IMPORTANT. How are you expected to complete every necessary task in your life if you didn't juggle three things at once?

Allow me to say – you won't. Saying you're too busy or too important or too reliable is the <u>ultimate</u> distraction. It gives us permission to set the creative life aside because the "real" world (full of its responsibilities) is more essential to our well-being and achievement than our creative self. *What is more "real" than the core of our creative being?*

> *Saying you are too busy is the ultimate distraction, permission to NOT try.*

I spent over thirty years as a management consultant, working with hundreds of companies to assist them in doing things better. For more than twenty of those years, I was also a university professor at the master's and doctoral levels and a faculty administrator and coach. Everyone wanted to do things "better". Everyone was important. Everyone was busy, including me.

Experience taught me one very critical lesson. Trying to do too much at one time means we do nothing as well as when we concentrate on one thing. In the moment. Deliberate. Fully and whole-heartedly. I am going to give you examples, and I'm betting you will relate to these in your heart of hearts.

A sidebar for a moment... For those of you with eagle eyes, you might have noticed that I didn't talk about one aspect of my mind-map seen at the beginning of Step 2 – inspiration. As I added branches to that boundaries and barriers topic, I realized *filling my creative well* was a major concept all by itself. Here's my map for it!

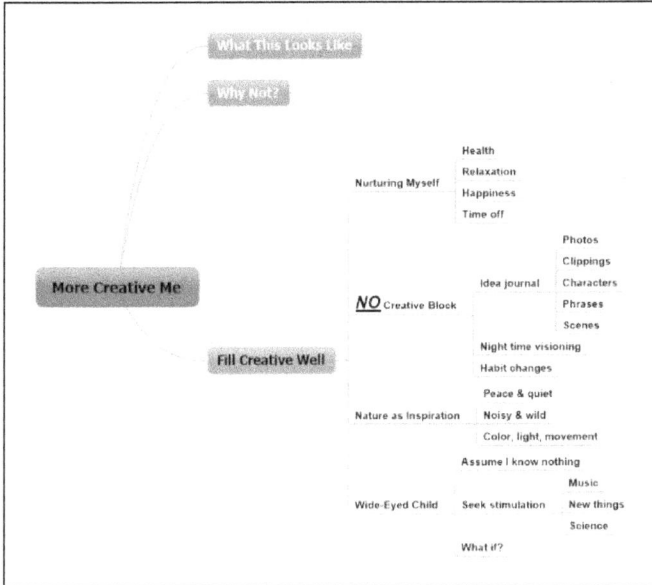

First, we'll talk about the stories we tell ourselves about it, and then, how to do it. Take notes as things occur to you for your own well-filling exercise later on.

> *Doing a couple of little things while we're busy*
> *with that big project – it won't hurt.*
>
> **NOT!!!**

BUSY LITTLE THINGS

You're working on that report (or paper, or book, or piece of art, or composition) and an email arrives. Someone asks you a question, and you know it won't take long to reply. Besides, a little mental break will do you good, and getting this out of the way will keep your mind clear.

EXCEPT...

The email response is more than a sentence or two, because we're polite and have to ask about the vacation/child's game/date night. Two sentences become two paragraphs. Then we share what's happening with us, because we're human and want to reciprocate in information sharing. At least another paragraph. Hit the send button. Then because we're there, we check to see if anything else important and urgent has arrived in ye ol' inbox.

Pretty soon, an hour has passed. An hour that we were supposedly dedicating to being creative.

> *Multitasking is an effective way to accomplish things.*
> **NOT!!!**

MULTITASKING MYTH

"I may as well listen to that business podcast while I'm on the elliptical machine." This applies to any kind of physical activity. It could be gardening, walking or exercise equipment. (I admit, I'm also guilty here.) First, we want to pass the time in a way we find to be beneficial. And sometimes, we distract ourselves because, to be honest, the task at hand is **BORING**. Who loves weeding the garden or cleaning the house? Anyone raising their hands?

We are crushed under the weight of feeling productive, even when we're doing something that does not otherwise require our minds. A podcast while I'm walking or a training video while I'm on the elliptical takes my mind off the drudgery of my body moving. I can weed up a storm without thinking about anything when I have earbuds in, listening to an audiobook.

And that's the point. I am not thinking. I'm in a zone of semi-engagement, and that does not bode well for filling my creative bucket. If mental downtime is your purpose, ask yourself this. Are you truly 'down' if you are distracting yourself with something else? Think about it. I'll wait....

Back now? What conclusion did you reach? Certainly the examples I used that included something related to personal or professional growth would not be downtime, because my brain was then engaged trying to learn something new. Listening to music makes us feel and listening to books presents us with new ideas.

But, you ask, "How will I get everything done if I don't multitask?"

The answer is, you might not. You might not finish listening to that new bestseller as fast as everyone else. You might have to wait a few days to absorb that photography tip or capture that phrase in Spanish. You might not listen to the whole album you just bought in one pass.

How important is that to you in weighing things for you best creative life?

> If you don't nurture yourself, no one else will do it for you.

NURTURING

The next piece of advice in filling your creative well is determining how you can nurture yourself. The care and feeding of YOU is as critical as that of your children/spouse/significant other, your friends, your job, and your social life. In fact, it's even more important, because if you aren't at your best, how can you give to others?

What are the most important things in your life? What could you be missing through distractions? How will you even know you're missing them?

This morning we took a long walk with the dogs. The weather was momentarily sunny and crisp between Pacific Northwest rain storms. February looms on the close horizon, and Mother Nature is making a point of telling us she might send us an early spring. My muscles felt the hill climbs, but I

was grateful I could walk them when some of
friends are not nearly as lucky anymore.

All of this I might have missed, had I not been **IN THE MOMENT**.

There was more, like a flock of geese numbering thousands circling overhead. I would have missed their honking, which is what alerted us to their whirling progress, if I'd been listening to anything on a headset. If I was distracted by listening to something that required me to puzzle out a problem, I might have missed the smile on my girl dog's face, the goofy one with her ears flat out like an old nun's habit and all her teeth showing with her big floppy tongue, telling me how pleased she was we'd made the time to hit the trail. The wonderful season would not have registered. I certainly would not be thinking about feeling grateful.

I would have missed out on a lot. Instead, my mind emptied and I enjoyed being in the moment, peaceful, quiet, silent. When we returned an hour later, I could jump into my writing routine more quickly because my mind had reset itself to a full tank of creative goodness.

If you are still skeptical, consider the times you are trying to remember an elusive fact. It could be a name. It could be a date or location. It's there, on the tip of your tongue, but you cannot spit it out. The harder you try to remember, the more likely you are to lose it altogether.

What makes you remember? Letting go. You quit trying so hard, or perhaps forget about the item, and suddenly <<POOF>> it pops into your mind. It needed a minute to locate the file. It's a crowded place, your mind, filled with the many things you have to do and – well, I don't want to browbeat you with more of the same.

BENEFITS OF REFILL

Just like a pitcher under a faucet, your creative well needs time to refill. The chief benefit is a full jug of energy to water your projects. Okay, you may find that analogy a little too cute, but it applies.

Perhaps the most thrilling benefit of filling your creative well is **avoiding creative blocks**. People who fill their wells find ideas – everywhere! It's because their subconscious spends its time on intake when their conscious brain is taking a break. Let me provide a few examples from a writer's perspective.

While on our walk, my subconscious took in the feel of damp air on my exposed skin, and how my cold fingers felt when I pulled them inside my sweatshirt sleeves. New grass is painfully green, almost to the point of hurting those who look at it. Wind whistles in trees, making the tops sway in time to their primitive

music. Rotting vegetation leaves a stench
behind that I can taste in the air. It could be
disgusting, except I know it brings the soil
needed nutrients that encourage more plants
to grow.

What did you notice? These sensory messages came courtesy of my subconscious, and I could recall them in an instant to write about them. All I had to do was close my eyes and let myself feel being on that walk, and the senses were there.

Every creative will experience this in a way that makes sense for them. For example, someone whose creative art is painting might find the memory of green grass intriguing. It's not just one green, but many hues and the shades change with the sun and shade. A chef might smell the wild onions by the creek and think about how the new growth of spring can be incorporated into a dish. A photographer would want a picture of those geese, their staggered v-shaped interlocking lines dark slashes against the clouds.

> *It's not enough to fill the creative well. We have to feel confident we can coax that well to run when necessary.*

TAPPING THE WELL

The well does not have faucets on it, one marked cold when we want a slow trickle and the other hot for a fast blast. If it was only that easy! We might not have a creative block, and the ideas would flow whenever we wanted them. It's the nature of the ideas and whether it's the right time to work on them that are another story.

> *Your muse lives in your subconscious mind. Memorize that address so you can visit it often.*

How do you access the creative jumping off point you want for a project? I write romantic suspense, psychological thrillers, and nonfiction creativity tips. I also blog and write newsletters, and I try to come up with something meaningful and inspirational to post on social media on a regular basis. Yes, I have ideas for all of them. But like snowfall in Chicago in July, it might not be the right time.

Accessing your creative idea bank is a skill you develop in a way that makes sense for you. You might have to try a number of these out before you find ones that work the best. Here are the prompts I use on a regular basis.

Idea Journals

I see new ideas everywhere, because I am a fly on the wall and observe no matter where I am. Honestly, we call it character-collecting and story-catching in my house!

I have electronic and paper folders with ideas, separated into broad categories. Over the years, I have found that it is best for me to put them in groups according to the genre or the topic or the book series. You will have categories that make sense for your unique creative process. Whatever taps the well!

My idea journals include photos of people, places and things. I cut clippings out of magazines, papers and blogs. I write down traits and characteristics I observe in human nature and behavior. I take photos of scenes and locations. I listen to how people say things, their phrasing, and I keep those too.

For clarification, I'll point out that when I say 'clip', it could be a cut-and-paste of a digital version, the old fashioned scissors and paper. Originally, everything was paper. Then I started adding some word processing files, but the compilation of all of the pieces got messy and disorganized. I hated not being able to find the clue I wanted, when I needed it most!

I have now been putting things into a software package designed for capturing both research and writing. I scan in a picture, and can write a short description of what strikes me about it. I can link in webpages and files, again including short descriptions. I can organize the contents into topical folders. I can even write in it, though I find it doesn't work as well for me – yet. Creative process is always a work in progress! If you're curious about what I'm using, drop me an email, or check out my website for recommendations on tools I use.

Visioning

Originally, I was going to call this 'night time visioning', but then I discovered a few new tricks…

Years ago, I had a very stressful job. My doctor's take on it was that it was going to kill me. I either had to learn to master the stress, or it would master me.

That led me to clinical hypnosis as a stress management mechanism. Yes, it worked for stress, but it also released an interesting aspect of my creative process. It helped me learn how to tap my creative well on cue.

(Hang in with me – there's a reason for my meandering…)

The process worked like this. When I was ready to fall asleep at night, I would think about the characters in whatever story I was working on. It wasn't a deliberate, this-is-what-they-do-next kind of thing. I just thought about them, as you might think about family or friends in an idle way at the end of your day. As I drifted off to sleep, they were on my conscious mind.

Then my subconscious took over. Somehow – and honestly, I don't think even brain science researchers or psychologists fully understand how this works – when I woke in the morning, the characters were there. More importantly, they could tell me where their story would go that writing day. Words flowed like proverbial rivers. And they were good words too, turning into good stories at a rapid rate.

Did you know that before electric lights and alarm clocks, most people had a period of creative wakefulness during the night?

It's true! Before we forced ourselves into a rhythm based on our ability to stay up late with artificial light and wake early to an irritating buzz, we humans fell asleep at night for a few hours, then woke for an hour or more, then fell asleep again. That middle of the night time was a very creative period.

When I decided to write full time, I dumped my alarm clock. I go to bed when I'm sleepy, thinking about characters or writing in general, and when I wake up in the middle of the night, I think about writing projects. I find new ways to explain ideas, or new twists to a plot. I keep a notebook by my bedside, and I jot down enough detail about my ideas so that I can pick up the thread in the morning.

And it works. Consistently, it works. Night visioning, coupled with sleep segmentation, feeds my creative capabilities.

I will fully admit that had someone explained this to me before, I would have been skeptical. I might have been willing to give it a try, but maybe not. I mean, we need our uninterrupted sleep. Eight hours a night and all that. We need rest for creativity. This is true, but we probably don't need as much rest as we believe we do, unless we have highly physical work during the day. Lots of brain bandwidth is another story.

And, by the way, the reason I dumped the 'night' part of this is I've found I can do this during the day too. Close my eyes, concentrate on the characters, and let my mind hum along at its own pace. Pretty soon, my subconscious comes through for me, sparking the muse into action.

Change Habits

This one will seem kind of – well – normal after my previous section! To fill your creative well, change your habits.

We all have those lists of things we "need" to be creative. Habits, whether they are tools or locations, sounds or silence, are things we've become used to as part of our creative process. But sometimes, to fill the well, you need to dismantle it first.

This does not have to be a big thing. It can be a small item, like shifting where you work, or when you work, or how. For me, original writing, as in adding new word count, had often been a morning pursuit. Not early morning, necessarily, but before my brain becomes engaged with countless other thoughts that are – yes, you guessed it – distractions!

But then, as part of my new regime, I had a commitment to exercise. My body benefits from it the most (and I am least likely to blow it off) if I exercise first thing in the morning.

Hhmmm... See my dilemma?

I decided to try something new to shake this up. Changing my early day writing habit, I decided I would write throughout the day, at any time. Early afternoon, evening, maybe even the middle of the night. I would tell myself that whatever the hour, it was my writing time, and I would write.

A funny thing happened. It worked! I find I can write at any time of the day. Furthermore, they're good words, fast words, powerful words. Words that don't end up in the recycle bin.

(Not being one to settle, I decided to see how far I could take this and tried it on exercise too. Yes, changing habits works here too!)

An important aspect to keep in mind when we try something different is that it can refresh us. It shakes up our process, which may spur new creative directions. A musician friend of mine tried this, changing her morning composing time to evening. She has a day job, and like many of us, she carries it home with her. She thought composing would help her decompress. What she found, though, is that the energy of her day translated into a new beat and energy in her music. It accessed a different part of her creative well.

Inspirational Resources

We all need outside stimulation from time to time. Even when we have a good idea we're excited about, we don't have the inspiration we need to put it into action. That's when we turn to our inspirational resources.

As you might have guessed based on previous sections, one of my inspirational resources is nature. I love being outdoors in a plant-related setting. I like to situate where I am working to view nature. The craziness of a storm is an upper for me, but I get a zap from sunny days too. Put me on a mountain or a beach, a lush forest or a rocky desert, and I find something inspiring in it.

When I need to pause and sort what my fingers type next, I look outside. My desk overlooks my garden as I type this. If I'm working in a coffee shop, I try to sit where I can see distant trees. If I'm in a city and I need my fix, I page through photos I've taken from natural settings.

Each of us has an inspirational resource that works for us. A painter friend swears by city noise. A writer uses bodies of water. A chef might want to sit in an array of aromas, and dancing might be the inspiration for a musician. What speaks to each of us only needs to make sense to us and no one else.

It could be a trigger for our senses or a place of escape. Peaceful or loud, colorful or full of movement, there is no one right answer except the ones that brings you meaning. Find your personal inspiration, and your creative well will run over with productivity.

Wide-Eyed Child

I will be the first to admit that it's been decades since I was an innocent child. To an innocent child, the world is full of possibilities and there are no limits. Wide-eyed with wonder, they don't have to ask why not. Their days are not filled with negatives but positives.

In my early adult years, I was, as most of us are, concerned about getting ahead and staying afloat. I wanted to excel in business, have a rich life of friends and love, and enjoy everything I could. I also knew I couldn't afford to do everything, either in time or money, and while having life changing experiences was high on my list, the bucket list was something I didn't even consider.

Reality can turn harsh, and all of us go through some challenges and even tragedies as we grow older and hopefully, wiser. Yes, been there, done that, and tore up the t-shirt because I hated it. I knew there had to be a better way. What I found was an attitude adjustment. I turned myself into the wide-eyed child.

What is it and how did I do it? It is a whole lot easier to let yourself react to the world than be active in directing how you deal with it. I had to train myself, and again, this feeds my creative process. I look at everything, and most particularly, situations that are lousy, through three lenses.

I assume I know nothing.

I seek stimulation.

I ask myself what-if?

Assuming we know nothing is harder than it sounds. We develop hard-won ideals about how the world should work. I mean, why can't everyone see what an idiot that politician is? How much evidence do they need to be convinced that the world is...? I've always done it this way, and this is the way that works.

You get my point.

When we let go of those limitations, though, the world is something fresh and new. We get the privilege of examining things without the blinders of our beliefs, and sometimes, we learn those beliefs are unfounded. Exhibit A – my writing time. Exhibit B – my exercise time. You can list your own now. I'll be right here.

Your list might be short or long. You might already have this skill, and I applaud you! Most of us need to relearn this level of innocence, suspending our limits in favor of opening our minds, and through that, our creative processes. Assume you know nothing and want to learn everything.

When you are confident of this, seek stimulation. It might be through a lesson, like a new language. It might be sounds or sights, or any other sensory trigger. Science is fun, as are games and magic tricks. We're lucky to live in a time when we have the world at our open door in the form of the internet. While we might stumble across misinformation, we can also learn many amazing new things too.

The what-if phase is where the real creative juices start flowing. I'll give you an example. I was working on a romantic suspense story and the male lead was too flat. He wasn't enticing. He wasn't inspiring. He wasn't interesting. Even I was bored writing him, and I could only cringe about what my readers would think. I wanted to kill him, but that doesn't happen with a lead in a happily ever after!

I stepped away from the story and assumed the wide-eyed child search for something to make me happy. Idly flipping through a magazine, I found an article about something that had nothing at all to do with my characters or their story in any way, shape or form. It was idle knowledge about ancient Rome and generations of families and how they were perceived by the general population as heroes, even as their king saw them as losers. Not the stuff of a contemporary romance.

Then it struck me. What if my hero hated himself? What if he had done something others saw as brave and noble but he believed to be wrong? What if he hid behind the façade of boringness as a way to fly under the radar?

Zing! Couple that with some secrets and secrecy, and I had a hero again. But if I hadn't been willing to suspend belief and try something new, he would have been a casualty of a delete button.

Try something different without any preconceived notion about where it might lead. Assume nothing, and try it. Let the situation guide you and you might find anew creative direction entirely.

Exercise 3: Filling Your Creative Well

Add all of the different ways you could fill your creative well to your mind-map. Be generous with yourself and don't hold back!

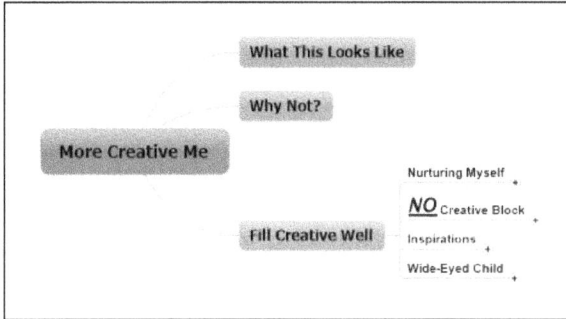

STEP 3 ON YOUR JOURNEY

To be creative, we need to have inspiration. These don't need to be BIG ideas, but many little ones. A color. A tone. A phrase. A dream. These exist in the creative well inside us, and just as someone drew a bucket from those country depths in the olden days, we need to lift our bucket of ideas. Next we'll discuss strategies to realize your best creative life.

STEP 4 – EMPLOY PRODUCTIVE STRATEGIES

As I noted before, **your creative journey is unique to you**. No one has walked in your shoes, following your path, with your life experiences. The strategies you use are therefore uniquely yours too. There are universal truths for your consideration, however. Adding on to our journey metaphor, I'll categorize these as stop signs, detours, missed turns, and directions.

STOP SIGNS

We rumble along on those old tires, the brakes squeaking each time we engage them. A gentle sway, the result of shocks long worn out, is something we don't even notice anymore. And if the wipers streak in each rainstorm, that's okay. It doesn't rain every day, right?

Just as the chariot for our journey should be in good working order, there are certain situations where we have things that should stop us, making us pause and reflect. Is this the right path? Are we ready? Are we doing what we should?

Or are we filling time with tasks that don't add to our creative body of work?

I'm the first to tell you that essentials such as feeding the family, washing the clothes, and balancing the bank account are all critical. Most of us also can be sucked into a long list of things that are not important, such as:

- Responding to social media or emails right this second

- Filing as a method of avoidance

- Cleaning your desk – unless you can't find things or are driven crazy by a few piles

- Phone calls at random times of the creative day

- Dusting the house (no, really, those dust bunnies are harmless)

Be honest. How often do you tell yourself you'll just check that one posting, and then realize you've not only wasted a chunk of creative time? You've also sucked the creative energy out of yourself. I'm as guilty of this as you are! As I write this paragraph, a large file is still being transmitted by my email server. Checking it every ten seconds will not make it go faster – and it wastes my time. (It doesn't make me feel anything other than more aggravated, either!)

What's Critical?

Guard your creative time as something precious, something you would not violate, except if someone you love was bleeding. (If you are bleeding, you should ignore that too.) Ask yourself, "What's critical for me to do next?" If the dust bunnies win, so be it. You might lose that creative window for the day, though.

Here's what I do. I make a list each day of what is critical for me to accomplish. Not everything makes it to that list, even if I have many other things that are important. But critical? My writing time. My exercise time. My social window with my hubby and our dogs. Other than that, all things are negotiable.

What's negotiable on your list? What are you doing to fill the time (because you think it won't take much?) What are you doing to avoid doing something that is critical in your creative life, but might be more difficult to tackle?

Priorities, people!

Some Assistance Required

Sometimes, we are driven crazy by the need to be two people, or three, or even four. There are so many responsibilities in our days, and we never seem to get to the one thing – the one critical creative thing – that would bring us the most joy. We try to do it all. We fail. We get frustrated, and that is NOT the road to greater creativity.

You've heard this one before. ASK FOR HELP. A writer I am friends with makes a big deal out of how important feeding her kids is each day. Home-cooked, from-scratch meals, which she plans, shops for, and cooks without relying on any pre-packaged ingredients. And she hates to cook!

Did I mention these children are teenagers? They have come to expect Mom to be at their beck and call for meals, to the point that even after she prepares something, if they don't feel like eating it, they expect an alternative. I hear you – she's set herself up for this, but come on, the kids should be able to cook for themselves by now.

Yes, yes, there are numerous lessons about boundary setting in this example. To clarify things, the busy Mom above will only draw the line in the kitchen coffee grounds when she's on a roll with her current work in progress and absolutely loves the direction it's going. If her writing is not progressing, the need to cook that from-scratch dinner is a great excuse to walk away from it.

Ask for what you need! In my experience, no one can read my mind, my well-hidden burning resentment, or my frustration – unless I'm throwing something or yelling. In those cases, I'm fairly clear, but by the time I've reached that point, any creative energy I have left was dissipated by the temper tantrum. Lay out expectations, and be willing to reciprocate. Your creative work can't ask for you.

Butts in the seat, fingers flying on the keyboard – or fretwork – or paintbrush. Whatever your creative medium, asking for the help we need to carve out our creative time is our responsibility.

And if *you* know how to read minds, please write a book about it and send it to me! I promise to give you a review in return!

> *If we don't change our ways, nothing will change.*

Reality Check

There's a bottom line to all of these activities. If we are trying to be creative at a time when we don't have creative energy, we'll grow to hate it. If we're trying to sandwich it in when we're distracted by a thousand other priorities, whatever we are able to accomplish under those conditions might not be that good, either.

Give yourself a reality check. It could be a time-out where you concentrate on why being creative is important to you. You might need to make some painful choices. None of us can do it all, I'm sorry to say. Trade-offs are necessary. Only you can decide how important this is for you.

For me, I get a little squirrelly if I'm not writing. Ditto if I'm not doing other creative tasks in my life, like designing and implementing a new garden or building a new recipe. I begin to blame 'things' for not having creative time, when it's me being my own worst enemy and not setting boundaries.

There are many things I don't do, because I want to create. I made choices. What choices are you willing to make?

DETOURS

We would all love to find ways to make things go better, faster, more easily. However, in most instances, creative

processes cannot be rushed. You can try them and see if you're part of the small minority who can get them to work, but for the most part, we need to put in the necessary time. Here's what can happen if we try to speed up a deliberate process.

Shortcut Temptation

I'm sure this has *never* happened to you, so I'll tell you about a time or six when it's happened to me. I need to travel from Point A to Point B by a certain time. My GPS system tells me I have plenty of time, and I believe it. I set out at the appointed time (with some extra built in, because that's me).

Then, as I make my way, something happens. An accident up ahead, or unexpected heavy traffic flows, or a bridge stuck in the upright position. But my handy, dandy GPS tells me it can find me an alternative route. I switch lanes and hit the exit ramp, delighted that I can cut off unnecessary wait time by trying that shortcut.

<<SCREECH>>. What shortcut? My freeway drive is now on surface streets. Stop, go, stop again. Oh look, a train track. Oh look, a freight train, and a long one by the look of it. That train is now stopping, and I am stuck in the middle of traffic on a one-way street. I turn the engine off, because it looks like I'm going to be here a while.

The message is shortcuts are rarely faster. You can't shortcut your creative process either. What's your strategy to allow the time necessary to make a creation you feel proud of?

Time Required

While you're thinking about shortcuts, think about the time required for your masterpiece too. Some of us have a very good idea of how 'fast' we can make our creative work. But if you don't...

Keep a journal or a log that reflects your creative medium and a realistic process. For example, for me, I know that when I'm taking photos for publication, there are multiple steps to the process. Taking the photos could be as simple as setting up a studio environment, or as complicated as a drive to a location and waiting for the right light and conditions. I would shoot a series, perhaps dozens of shots at different settings and angles, just to get one usable photo. Then there's adjusting it back at my computer.

For writing, it's word count. How fast can I write a fiction piece? How about nonfiction? (For me, they required different thinking processes and are not equal in terms of time.) It's still words, but they flow differently depending on what I'm writing. Some days, even the genre can flow differently.

In either example, I keep a log. For word count, I keep a small calendar on my desk, and I note which piece I worked on, for how long, and how many words I got. I journal in a notebook for photography. In both cases, I can then calculate how long it would take me to complete a project.

It's an estimate, of course. Every creative process can fall victim to delays, whether it's becoming stymied by an idea or blocked by a character or stopped by uncooperative subjects or light. I plan for the delays as well, but when it comes to the rough original work, I have become good at projecting how long something will take to accomplish.

Formulate your own data-grounded estimates. When you next carve out your creative time, you'll have a better idea of how much you can accomplish in the time you have allotted. Knowledge is power, and it also relieves us from beating ourselves up with unachievable expectations!

Patience

Yes, it's a virtue and all that stuff. Learn to practice it. Most of that comes down to two things – planning and permission.

The planning part is related to knowing how long something will take you, from a realistic perspective. It also means you must plan, not hope and pray that you'll somehow find the time in among everything else to maybe do it. Kind of. When you plan, you at least know that you have time to work on it, even if you don't complete it due to the aforementioned patience gremlins.

Permission is all on you. Give yourself permission to do the best you can. I can write 2000 words in an hour, and they're good words. But some days, my head is not as clear as I'd like or the characters aren't talking to me. (I hate it when they're having a hissy fit and I'm on the receiving end of it.) Or I am interrupted in a way that I could not guard against.

It may not be 2000 words, or they might be garbage. But I give myself permission to have days like that (just not often). I cannot be perfect every day. Maybe you can. Please write a book about how you do it. You will sell millions of copies!

Organized to Work

No matter how well you plan to work, if you are not prepared for your work session, it will not be successful. This detour is within our control. But sometimes it's easier to use disorganization as a method of avoidance.

Here's an example. You compose music. To do so, you use your guitar. But your guitar needs new strings, and you have not yet purchased those. And you need to string them once you get them. And tune the instrument. You might want to compose, but first you need to create the setting where you will do it.

I have another version of that. I get distracted if my desk is messy. Piles of papers waiting to be filed drive me nuts. Granted, my idea of messy is probably other people's ideas of neat and clean, but this is me. And it's all about me (in my case). What's your version of this?

There's a writer's version of this that's very popular to discuss. Internet connectivity. You hum along on work count when you realize you need a name for a secondary character. SCREECH! Wait, I'll open up a search browser and locate a site with given and surnames of the ethnic background of my character.

Half an hour later, you're fascinated by the history of old (whatever) names and their derivations, but you have not yet selected one, and you haven't written any more either. Put a placeholder word or symbol in your document so you can return to the section, and keep writing. I use a string of dollar signs to mark the spot and CAPITAL LETTERS to remind me what I need to do.

If you need to organize your creative space or look up ancient or modern facts, do it on non-creative time. You know when that is, the times when your brain is mush and your creative juices are sludge – or frozen solid. I find that right after lunch, my brain does not like to function. It's a wonderful time to file and research, though. Kind of like repetitive humming in the background of my mind…

If you need to buy paints or brushes, set up your studio, or tab your research materials, do it. Be prepared for your creative time, so you can make it as functional as possible.

Time Schedules

I am not a big fan of routines, at least, not for me. I also have many tasks I need to accomplish in a day. Setting a specific time to write or to exercise, the same time period each day, makes me crazy. It's not the way I function, though I know many people love that regularity.

Even though I don't like a set time slot doesn't mean I don't like to plan, however. There's a sureness to setting blocks of time in my calendar to perform certain activities. It means that I know I will get things done, since I have set the time aside for them as religiously as I set time for outside meetings and appointments. Here's my example from today.

7-9 am	*Check emails and social media, complete another lesson in a class I'm taking, eat breakfast*
9-10 am	*Work in the garden before the rain begins – again*
10-11 am	*Elliptical workout*
11am-1 pm	*Lunch, laundry, chores, meditation*
1-3 pm	*Work on the creative book (this one)*
3-5 pm	*Prepare media kit for nonfiction website*

Best laid plans and all that... The garden took longer than I anticipated, in large part because I ran into problems I could not have foreseen. However, this also produced a whole lot more physical labor than I thought it would too. Gardening took longer, and I didn't need the elliptical once I was done.

Now I'm working on the creative book. We'll see if I finish drafting it before my time slot is up. That's my plan. If I'm close, I'll run over, because completing the draft was a big priority for my day. And I don't think the media kit will take two hours.

What have you noticed about my plan? I engage in the priorities of my day – writing and exercise – as well as the business side of being an author – social media, media kit and website. All of those are priorities in my day.

The parts I don't put in the calendar are my personal time. My husband and I have coffee before we each grab our laptops and go for it at 7 am. We both work from home, so we spend lunch together. Any time after 5 pm is our space to fill. It's a healthy balance that works for us, and I have come to realize that as much as I'd LOVE to work 12-plus hours in the day as I used to, my executive function poops out a lot earlier than my intentions.

Some days, I may write for eight hours. Other days are filled with the business side. It all depends on what has the highest priority in the day.

I hope you noticed something else too. Despite the fact that I have set the time in my calendar for different activities, I'm not ruled by it. Flexibility is key. If I know the overtime on a task still won't get me to a daily goal, as in finishing a draft, I'll play with the schedule the next day to see how I can work it in. Found time, time left over after a task is completed, is reserved for simple things like household chores or reading a blog I had scanned earlier but didn't have time to read.

By planning my day, I avoid detours that could flatten the tires of my best intentions. Sure, emergencies happen. But at least I have a safe sense that I can complete the work and life activities I intend to by the end of the day.

MISSED TURNS

Like detours, missed turns are things we start doing almost unconsciously, but are not truly helping us complete our goals for the day. And they are oh-so-easy to turn into truckload-sized distractions. They fall under the broad categories of misdirected energy, vague directions, and changed courses.

Misdirected Energy

Did you ever hear a version of this?

"I made my 37 decisions for today, and I don't have another one in me."

It turns out it's true! Maybe your number is not 37 – could be more, could be less, could vary from day to day. I'm talking about executive function, the ability we each have to make decisions, plan our time, and implement difficult (mindful) tasks.

How much we have depends on many factors. Did you sleep well last night? Are you carrying around a chunk of worry about something you cannot control? Are you eating properly? Is exercise part of your agenda?

It's life, people. We don't always realize how many decisions we make in the course of a day. Many of them happen so fast, we never see them speed by. Others cause us to dither, uncertain or worried, until we are forced to act.

The more we can set up so that we don't have to decide on the fly, the better.

But wait, Yvonne. You said you don't like routine. Isn't setting things up so you know what comes when in a routine?

Sort of. The kind of set up I'm talking about is spending a few minutes at the end of your workday planning what you will work on the next day. For example, when I'm coming into the home stretch of completion writing a novel, I am *on fire*. I can't wait to finish it, not because – whew, it's done. It's because I see the climax and resolution for the characters, and they are screaming in my head to get it out there!

I may also have a blog post due, or an article for someone, or myriad other writing projects. We're not even thinking about running the business side, or my personal life. But gee, those characters…

I may set aside the whole day to write. I also determine what two or three things I want to complete in that day. I already know how fast I can write, so I can determine where I should be on word count before I close out one project and move to another. The temptation to favor one over another will still be there, but I stick to my plan as closely as possible.

Contrast this with wasting my energy. I know I want to finish that novel, and I need to edit the blog because I should post it by tomorrow. There are phone calls I need to make for the business. And on and on. Soon, too soon, I have used up my executive function on things that don't feed my creative side, the part where I can make money.

To make sure I get the most out of my day, I avoid anything that smacks of a decision for as long as possible. The phone calls each require me to consider how I'm going to respond on a call, when the other person asks me for something. Move that to the end of the day.

For me, editing requires less executive function than writing. (This is not the same for everyone – find your creative balance point.) I therefore move the editing to later in the day, because I need that executive function to be sharp for new words. I avoid email and social media altogether, at least until I have reached my other priority goals for the day.

Concentrating on tasks that require executive function until I run out of it allows me to wring the most creative energy out of my day. If you have less flexibility in your day, you'll have to be creative to be creative.

> *If you can control it, find a system so that you aren't using up your juice on things that aren't feeding your creative process.*

Vague Directions

What if you don't know what creative project you're working on next? You're out of ideas, sense of adventure, and fun. This can happen in the midst of a project too. You're puttering along, all engines firing and the project becoming a masterpiece, until you're not.

This strategy could just as easily be called, "Creative, Know Thyself". Each of us develop work habits from our life experiences. I was a management consultant for years, and I always had files of project strategies, tools and processes that I found interesting, but did not apply to the clients I worked with at that time.

To this day, I still keep files of ideas. I see a face I like, or read about a person with interesting characteristics. They go into a file. I take a picture of a location that inspires me. I find a science blog fascinating. Maybe any and all of these things will find their way into a book. Or a blog. Or an article.

Or nothing at all.

Another of my work habits is self-directed time. I had my own management consulting practice, and I worked from home for decades. I was also a university professor for decades, and for the most part, I taught remotely or online. In any of these roles, I had to rely on me, myself and I to get'er done. Yes, I had clients and students and administration with expectations, but the onus was on me to complete my work.

No one looked over my shoulder, which turned me into a driven boss of myself. I think this is why I can stay organized, on track, and results-oriented. It is not a work style that is for everyone. If you are someone who thrives on last minute deadlines, it won't be for you!

Finally, I know certain non-work activities help me to relax, tickle my subconscious for ideas, and restock my supply of executive function. From experience, I know I get great ideas for blog posts while I exercise. All I need is a title and I can run with it. Cooking even a simple meal takes me to place of mental replenishment. Gardening equals absolute relaxation.

I'm sharing this with you not because I expect you to be the same. No, the lesson here is learning about your work habits, your inner self, and your creative process. It's about creating positive means to restart a sidelined project, pull out your creative tools when you least want to, or find the mechanism that makes you want to be creative once more.

Changing Course

Missed turns can be of our own making, even in a subconscious way. Something works very well for you, until it doesn't any more. But it's been working, so we carry on, sure that somehow, in some miracle way, things will get back on track.

Don't be afraid to change what isn't working. This does not mean trying something for a day and throwing it out. Give it a decent try. When I was a child, I wanted to take lessons and learn lots of different things, like musical instruments, art, and sports. My parents would tell me they would be happy to pay for whatever it was, as long as I gave it the time it deserved. Enough lessons, putting in practice, and sticking with it until I could prove, one way or the other, that it was a good or bad fit. Sometimes that was a few months, and sometimes it was a year, but we always knew how long I was going to try.

Try something new. Make a pledge to yourself to try it for long enough to be sure it doesn't fit you before you jettison it. In the process, you might find great fits that add to your creative process in ways you cannot yet imagine.

GUIDEPOSTS

No matter how smart and talented we are, we all need guideposts to help us on our creative journey. Yes, innate artistic talent helps. The right eye helps. Being a natural storyteller helps. But we can all be better, even if we're good-to-great now. We still need road signs.

You can read the creative map by asking experts, following leaders, reading instructions, and learning to read one-way signs.

Expert Wisdom

No matter who we are or what our creative medium, someone walked that path before us. It might have been long ago, or minutes. It might be for only seconds, before they veer off in a different direction. They may tread lightly or stomp their feet. But someone is an expert in what you need to know.

As a photographer, I have long been in awe of *National Geographic* pictures. The topics! The locations! The stories told in color – or in black and white! How did that photographer know to be in just that place, at just that time, with just that setting?

A few years ago, I was lucky enough to meet a retired *Nat Geo* camera guy, and like kids at the feet of Mister Rogers, I wanted to learn everything he knew. Most of it turned out to be things like this.

Do your homework about your subject, as in, learn what will make photos of this subject unique. Then learn when you could get those shots. Prepare your gear and your person.

Then wait for it. Patience, not my best virtue!

In this age of digital, he also shared something amazing. He worked before the digital age, and he said that often, he would shoot a full roll of film, 36 exposures, and have maybe – *maybe* – one shot that was decent! It's nice to have the ability today to delete the shots that clearly don't work.

I study things about places I'm going, in case I stumble across that great, unique perspective. I plan for them, when I can. And I still shoot – a lot and with many different settings, because it isn't always clear how something will turn out. Serendipity is an amazing thing! I would have taken a couple of variations and called it good before.

I never would have known without sitting at the master's feet.

Mimicry

Leaders are out there in your creative medium. Like the photographer I talked about above, they are willing to share their knowledge. You see, most of them remember an important fact. They are learners too. In fact, scratch the surface of most experts and you find students too.

Sometimes, though, it isn't enough to ask for their advice. You need to try it yourself. Okay, so my shots may not – yet – win any awards, but I've taken some good ones, things I could sell, things people admire. I keep studying the masters, taking classes, and practicing – lots of shooting.

Are you discouraged? Don't be. No matter what we're known for now as a creative, and no matter where you are in your development, you had to begin someplace. Pull out some of your first paintings, or spun yarn, or short story. Don't criticize it. *Analyze* it as the starting point of your journey to where you are today. If you are honest with yourself, you'll see glimmers of hope, early skill, and genius. It's there. Look closer, and celebrate the distance you've traveled so far.

And practice, practice, practice. There's an enticing path leading to your creative future for you to follow.

Instructions

No matter what we do as creatives, there are rules or directions we need to follow. If you don't let the paint dry long enough, your masterpiece could be ruined in transit. If you don't have good grammar skills, readers will throw your work aside. A low-pixel photo will be blurry once enlarged. These are what I would call the absolutes.

There are many other instructions, though, that fall more in the category of sound advice. What's in style? This matters if you want to sell something! Yes, create something that is meaningful for you, but you might not sell it right now. Styles change, though, and someday, down the road...

In the writing world, self-publishing was considered a vanity a few years ago. You only did it if you knew your work would never be picked up by a publisher. Finding that traditional publisher fell under the magic of agents, so you first had to appeal to an agent, who then had to sell the work to a publisher. Then the editor needed to like it...

Some people still consider a traditional publishing contract as the sign they have arrived. Look at the bestseller lists today, and you will find things have changed. There are no guarantees one method is better than the other. Both have merits and value, and both have challenges.

Instructions on how to proceed in each arena boil down to one common rule or instruction – write a good story (or nonfiction topic).

Each field has its own set of instructions. Learn the ones that apply to you – and the ones you can think about ignoring.

No One Way

No matter what we create, we have to learn how to create a recipe for our own success. Unique, individual, special, ours.

Yes, the experts can provide wisdom and we can imitate our heroes, but despite the instructions and advice, there is no one way to do things.

Exercise 4: Strategies to be Creative

Add to your mind-map for the strategies you will implement to be creative. Here is a reminder of possible strategies to consider.

What This Looks Like

Why Not?

Fill Creative Well

More Creative Me

Strategies to be Creative

Stop Signs	Ask what's critical	
	Ask for help	
	Reality check	
Detours	Short cuts don't work	
	Time is required	
	Patience is vital	
	Be organized to do work	
	Block time for work	
Missed Turns	What do I like doing?	
	Accommodate my work habits	
	Change courses as necessary	
Guideposts	Positive triggers	
	Experts	
	Thought leaders	
	Instructions	
	No "one way"	

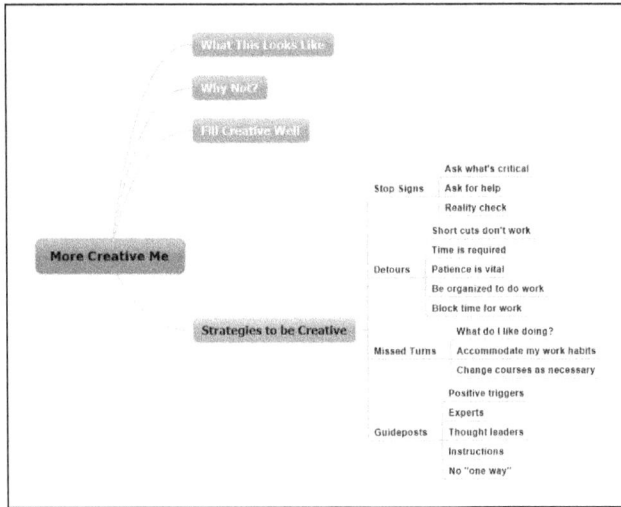

There is no single set of creative guidelines for you to follow, except TO TRY. Show up, do your work, try new things, dump things that aren't working for you. Experiment, take risks, rage when you are not the winner selected, then learn from the experience.

You have it in you, you know. You are a creative. You will conquer your fears, destroy your demons, and find your hidden masterpiece!

STEP 4 ON YOUR JOURNEY

I've suggested strategies that I've implemented in my creative life. Many are common to creatives across mediums. Pick things you want to work on. (They can be easy things. Nothing like a little success to make you want to try another something new!) Make your measure of "success" something measurable that YOU can identify and "see" in a definitive way. Next, a polemic about how to implement your creative life.

How to Implement Your Creative Life
OR
How to Climb the Mountain Daily

By now, your head is probably spinning and you're asking, "Yvonne, how do I DO THIS???"

I understand both your pain and your feeling of being overwhelmed. How much you implement depends on the time you have and how much effort you can reasonably dedicate to being a more creative you. Here's my recommendation.

Flip back through the chapters, and find two or three things that resonated with you. You might have marked a passage or remember an idea. Write them down.

Now select one that will be the easiest for you to try. Got it?

Then try it for long enough to understand how it helps you.

Then add the second and try them both together for a time. Then the third.

Roll with it for a while, and see what kind of difference it makes in your creative life. If something isn't working after you've given it a healthy try, select something else. You'll find the mix that works for you!

> *We create for the joy of being creative. If we*
> *try to fool ourselves with any other reason,*
> *there will be no joy.*

I do try to practice what I preach! Some days are more challenging than others. I have the same "stuff" in my life as you have in yours – illness and injury, family issues, a difficult boss (that's when I can be found lecturing myself!) Still, I wouldn't give up being a creative in *just this way* and at this point in my life's experience for anything in the world! (Well, maybe that big lottery prize...)

To "climb the mountain daily, Here's what I do:

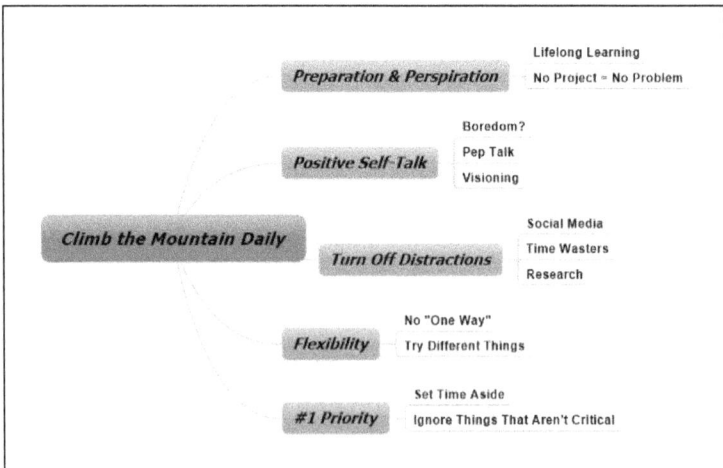

Climb the Mountain Daily

Preparation & Perspiration
- Lifelong Learning
- No Project = No Problem

Positive Self-Talk
- Boredom?
- Pep Talk
- Visioning

Turn Off Distractions
- Social Media
- Time Wasters
- Research

Flexibility
- No "One Way"
- Try Different Things

#1 Priority
- Set Time Aside
- Ignore Things That Aren't Critical

PREPARATION AND PERSPIRATION

I study my craft continuously. I always learn something new, too. Like many artistic mediums today, things change rapidly. Perhaps it's not about the craft but about the business around the craft. Social media is the perfect example, and that applies to all of us creatives! I learn about what's happening in my genres, how to be a better writer, and where I should take my business next.

I also give myself a break if I face a period when I *DO NOT* have the energy to be creative. Like it or not (humans again), when life deals us a particularly bad blow – death, sickness, fire or flood, business collapse – it is hard to stay on course. Give yourself permission to take time off for good behavior – or bad luck. OR turn it into your next masterpiece. I find there is something I can learn from any situation, good or bad, that can fuel a creative spurt.

Finally, if you aren't really sure about your skills and capabilities, do an honest self-assessment of your creative craft. What benchmarks should you set for your achievements? Are they too advanced based on where you are in your creative career? What gaps in knowledge do you need to fill? Being honest and cataloging where you are and where you need to go provides you with a map for the lifelong learning part of your creative journey.

> *Rid yourself of self-imposed creative*
> *limitations.*

Positive Self-Talk

Pep talks, affirmations, daily meditation – this goes by a number of names. Whichever you prefer, give yourself a boost every day. Positive language, the repetition of things that are right and good instead of saying what you will avoid, can go a long way toward framing your subconscious into a creation-making machine. Here are some examples.

Don't say – "I won't let myself watch season one of XXX until I finish my word count."

DO SAY – "I will write 2000 words during my awesome creative hours today."

Don't say – "I'll only take that walk around the park after I take care of everyone else's needs."

DO SAY – "I'll set time in my calendar to take a walk around the park so that I am refreshed to take care of my family's needs."

You get the idea. I also ask myself if I am making excuses about not being creative because I'm bored with what I'm working on. It happens, and I know it's not just to me! Like heading to the fridge for a snack when you aren't hungry (boredom eating), you can think up boredom distractions too. Does that load of laundry *really* need to be folded now, or can it wait until you've spent another half hour on this canvas?

Part of my self-talk is visualization too. I imagine what it will be like to…whatever creative success I would like to achieve. It could be fixing a story's messy pacing problem or designing a social media campaign that will resonate with people, or anything else you can think of for your best creative life. If I think about this right before I drift off to sleep, my subconscious plays with it overnight and when I wake, I find I have an answer. Try it – you'll like it!

Turn Off Distractions

I've spent quite a few words on this topic already, but I'll add one more point for your consideration. Have you seen the grid of important and urgent?

Urgent, Not Important	**Important AND Urgent**
Not Urgent, Not Important	Important, Not Urgent

All of us operate out of each of these boxes at different times, and for varying reasons. For your creative life, you will accomplish the most if you can set priorities in creativity that fill the **Important AND Urgent** checkbox. That's *important* for your progress on the creative journey, and *urgent* in feeding your creative soul.

Other distractions include things that waste our time, things we decide to do because they are excuses, giving us permission to avoid being creative. (This is NOT the kind of permission I was discussing earlier!) As important as effective use of social media can be to promoting our creative work, most of us are probably guilty from time to time of watching videos that don't aid our creative power *or* relax us in lieu of our creative life.

A final distraction – research. Writers, we know we're guilty of this! Our work might be tooling along like a well-running sports car when we suddenly hit the brakes because we MUST know how many moons Jupiter has or what kind of food-conveying utensils would be on a poor man's table in 18th century China. Artists, do you have enough of that color to finish your creative time TODAY? THEN you can order more! Live in the creative moment, and put a placeholder like ??? in to remind you to look things up when you've already achieved your creative goal for the day.

Flexibility
There is no "one way" to do things. Thinking there is only one way is like only turning left in a city of one-way

streets. You will go in circles and unless your destination is inside those blocks, you aren't going to get there! Be flexible and try new things. Make new things a habit, and you might discover even **Better** ways of achieving your creativity goals.

Set Your Creativity as a Major Priority

No one can do it but you. No creativity fairy will sprinkle magic dust on your head and take away your boundaries and barriers. No ogre will wrestle your time back for your creative life. No one will convince your subconscious that you can do it if you don't. Ignore the things that aren't critical and give yourself permission to create.

Remember...

"Creativity is contagious. Pass it on."

Albert Einstein

THE END

AND THE BEGINNING OF YOUR BEST CREATIVE LIFE!

Also by Y J Kohano/Yvonne Kohano

GOOSE YOUR MUSE

Four Steps to Being a More Creative You

Four Steps to Business Planning for Plan-Phobic Creatives

Four Steps to Building Your Creative Market

MIND WEB PSYCHOLOGICAL THRILLER SERIES

Mind Stalked, Book 1

Mind Etched, Book 2

Mind Tangled, Book 3

FLYNN'S CROSSING ROMANTIC SUSPENSE SERIES

Pictures of Redemption, Book 1

Flashes of Fire, Book 2

Naked Intolerances, Book 3

Tastes and Consequences, Book 4

Blooms on the Bones, Book 5

Wine Into Water, Book 6

Love and the Christmas Tree Nymph, A Flynn's Crossing Seasonal Novella

Love's Touch of Justice, Book 7

This Proposal Between Us, A Flynn's Crossing Seasonal Novella

Measure Twice, Love Once, Book 8

Love's Fiery Prescription, Book 9

Love's Fiery Resolution, Book 10

And more to come!

Learn about upcoming releases at www.YvonneKohano.com.

Please leave an honest review of this nonfiction work at your favorite book discovery site of choice. I love to hear from readers, so feel free to contact me directly on Facebook as Yvonne Kohano, on Twitter @yvonnekohano, and at yvonne@yvonnekohano.com.

About the Author

Award winning storycatcher Y J Kohano/Yvonne Kohano writes contemporary romantic suspense, psychological thrillers, and nonfiction tips on creativity, when she's not gardening, cooking, traveling, reading or learning something new. Follow her at www.YvonneKohano.com (psychological thriller and romantic suspense fiction), www.GooseYourMuse.com (creativity tips), and Facebook and Twitter to learn what tickles her about being a writer.

www.ingramcontent.com/pod-product-compliance
Lightning Source LLC
Chambersburg PA
CBHW061753020426
42331CB00006B/1457